LARRY GARLAND

CONNECTING MEN TO MEN THROUGH CHRIST
Published in Harrisburg, Pennsylvania,
by Impact Communications

Copyright © 2010 by Larry Garland

ISBN: 978-0-9829879-0-2

Unless otherwise indicated, Scripture quotations are from:

The Holy Bible, King James Version

Printed in the United States of America

All rights reserved. Written permission must be secured from the publisher to use or reproduce any part of this book, except for brief quotations in critical reviews or articles.

First Edition: IMPG8-27-2010A00000

"May the God who gives endurance and encouragement give you a spirit of unity among yourselves as you follow Christ Jesus so that with one heart and mouth you may glorify the God and Father of our Lord Jesus Christ."

Romans 15: 5-6 (NIV)

"But he that is greatest among you will be your servant."

Matthew 23:11

Contents

Dedication	8
Testimonials	9
Forward	12
Introduction	13
SECTION 1 – INSPIRATION	17
The Big Picture Vision	18
The Vision of Men's Ministry	19
Embracing the Vision	20
Expanding the Vision	21
SECTION 2 – INVITATION	23
It Begins With a Small Group of Men	24
Connecting as Companions	25
Understanding the Mission	26
A Matter of Prayer	27
SECTION 3 – INFORMATION	29
Setting Their Hearts	30
Running the Race	31
Passing the Baton	32
Staying on Target	33
SECTION 4 – INTEGRATION	35
Balancing Their Lives	36
Raising the Standard	37
Growing in Grace	38
Proving Their Faith	39
Progressing in Ministry	40
SECTION 5 – IDENTIFICATION	41
Continuing the Vision	42
Laying the Foundation	43
Shepherd / Leader Oversight	44
Relationship Development	45
Taking the Initiative	46

SECTION 6 – INTERDEPENDENCE — 47
Setting the Pace — 48
Experiencing Their Giftedness — 49
Leading by Example — 50
Realizing Their Potential — 51

SECTION 7 – IMPLEMENTATION — 53
Following a Plan — 54
Environments for Investment — 55
The Huddle — 56
The Summit — 57
Connecting in Focus Groups — 58

SECTION 8 – INTERACTION — 59
Instruction and Discussion — 60
Acceptance and Encouragement — 61
Christ-Centered Lifestyles — 62
Sharing Their Stories — 63
Building Friendships — 64
Prioritizing God's Word — 65
Growing in the Process — 66

SECTION 9 – INVESTMENT — 67
Refocusing the Vision — 68
The Locker Room — 69
Finding Their Roles — 70
A Matter of Choice — 71

SECTION 10 – INFLUENCE — 73
Celebrating a Friendship — 74
Philosophy for Changed Lives — 75
Profile for Shepherd / Leader Mentoring — 76
Profile for Shepherd / LeaderDiscipleship — 77
Perception of a Shepherd / Leader — 78

SECTION 11 – INVOLVEMENT — 79
Rising to God's Call — 80
Pleasing the Father — 81
A Defining Moment — 82
A Divine Appointment — 83

Contemplating the Call	85
A Matter of Perspective	86
SECTION 12 – INSTRUMENTS	87
Visions and Dreams	88
Standing Together	89
Preparing the Battle	90
Fulfilling His Purposes	91
SECTION 13 – INFILTRATION	93
Entering the Arena	94
Engaging the Opposition	95
Encountering the Opposition	96
Enduring the Opposition	97
Faith…Obedience…Sacrifice	98
Exiting the Arena	99
SECTION 14 – INTROSPECTION	101
Finishing the Race	102
Reflecting on the Mission	103
Delivering the Message	104
A Personal Decision	105
A Difference Maker	106
SECTION 15 – ILLUMINATION	107
Beginning the Connection	108
Completing the Connection	109
Leaving a Legacy	110
Rejoicing in Hope	111
Before the Throne	112
INTERVENTION: Rise Up	113
Recommended Reading	114
About the Author	115

Dedication

This book is dedicated to those men whose friendships I value and have both enriched my life and enlarged my capacity to follow God's call on my life as a Christian man. To each of you who have contributed in one way or another, I thank you for the privilege of serving together unto the glory of the gospel of our Lord Jesus Christ.

This book is also dedicated to all those men interested in a more meaningful walk with Jesus Christ and who are interested in the next steps in ministering to men. As our Connecting Men to Men ministry has grown, we desire as a team to encourage and support men from other churches as God would give us opportunity.

Testimonials

As I have watched and listened to Larry, as well as attended several of the Connecting Men to Men ministry events at his home church in recent years, including a three-day retreat, he clearly has convictions, a plan, and a worthy message that is bearing fruit. From my perspective, I see a man who has paid his dues in the formation of a men's ministry over a number of years and seems to have a special calling in leading men. Any Christian man who desires to grow in his relationship to Christ and/or aspires to build a thriving ministry to men should read this book.

Sam Lamonto, Lay Leader
Shiremanstown United Methodist Church
Shiremanstown, PA

As a result of their time and training with Jesus, the original twelve disciples were inspired to an uncommon commitment to Him that serves as a model for us as "ordinary" Christian men of today. Using numerous scriptural passages as a foundation to inspire similar heart development, Larry provides a very practical and transferable overall plan designed to grow a man's faith in service to God and other men. His step-by-step approach, designed to disciple men's hearts, is challenging, well organized, and would be a valuable asset for both personal growth as well as for ongoing ministry to men.

Jerry Cook, Lay Leader
St. John Lutheran Church, York, PA

The Connecting Men to Men ministry and the message of this book has clarified my purpose as a man and given me effective influence because it's all about God. I now see an active God as His Word triggers the Spirit to flow in and through myself and others. The Lord took me off the bench and put me on the playing field as an integral part of the varsity team.

Mark Craver, Layman
Church of the Open Door, York, PA

Today, Connecting Men to Men is a growing ministry that was initially ignited by the working of the Holy Spirit in the hearts of a small group of ordinary men. Together, functioning as a team, God has inspired an increasing number of men to accept the biblical challenges included in this book to be more godly in their leadership roles as men in their homes, at work, and within the church body.

Dale Stough, Layman
Church of the Open door, York, PA

I have known Larry for approximately three years. He has a great passion and heart for discipling men. It was evident the day I spoke to his church's men's group, and it is obvious that he has devoted much time and energy to overseeing events as well as developing programs and tools that help men grow their faith.

Don Schin, Master Licensee
ActionCOACH Business Coaching
Camp Hill, PA

In September 2008, Larry asked to speak at a Men's Summit Retreat. This event was well planned with an excellent balance of presentations, reflection time, recreational time and fellowship-bonding time. I loved the candor and atmosphere that permitted men to "safely" share their personal struggles and challenges. I left the retreat inspired and encouraged to a closer walk with the Lord. As I have been given opportunity to preview this book, I anticipate similar blessing from God that would increase my usefulness to bring Him glory among those men most often in my sphere of influence.

Joseph Robinson Jr., Author and Speaker
Harrisburg, PA

Foreword

What an honor and a blessing to share what I know about my dear friend and brother in Christ, Larry Garland. To watch and listen to Larry as he wrote this book was to witness him growing in courage and in the power of the Holy Spirit. He has often reminded me that, although Bible studies are very important, men's ministry has to be more than a mere Bible study to accumulate an excessive amount of irrelevant information or even useful knowledge without practical application. Men's ministry should be viewed as an opportunity to gather in a variety of environments, whereby deeper, Christ-centered friendships are established with other Christian brothers. Uniquely encouraged by other men, they are equipped to live out their faith in a more strategic and purposeful way. The real issue becomes, as part of the challenge of 1 Peter 5:1-5, to be men who are humble, teachable, and both eager and willing to shepherd God's flock. Are we in a place or relationship with other men that allows the Holy Spirit opportunity to reproduce and multiply the life of Christ in and through us as part of a team? I found Larry's book to offer many excellent thought patterns that have proven to be very practical without being performance driven, and I am very thankful for the high priority that is given to scripture as the means to communicate what he perceives is a God-honoring vision and message for men. While his book offers many biblical principles for personal growth, I believe it was the challenge and encouragement to be a functional part of a team that has brought about the most notable change in my life.

John Langel
Executive Books
Mechanicsburg, PA

Introduction

As Christian men, we are encouraged to view our lives like a personal journey with Jesus Christ, ultimately that ends with us leaving this world to live with Him in heaven, hopefully, leaving a godly legacy for others to follow in our absence. Many of us have been down the road far enough to realize that this journey is no easy task, but along the way demands different degrees of faith, obedience, and sacrifice if we are to impact the lives of others in a manner that will bring Christ the greatest glory. With this in mind, it is my desire that this book will inspire and equip you as a man, both as an individual and as part of a team, to "Rise to God's Call"; to faithfully persevere making disciples amidst a new generation of men till we all stand before Him at our journey's end.

Two thousand years ago, Jesus invited twelve ordinary men to follow Him on a journey like no other. As He would invest time building relationships with them, their commitment to Him would become both uncommon and undeniable as they would all die for their allegiance to Him (except for John, who would live out his days in exile). During a short span of three years, something extraordinary happened as they sat around the campfires with Jesus late at night, as He taught them lessons on and near the Sea of Galilee, and among the people in the synagogues and the villages, and as they gathered from time to time on the hillsides. Ultimately, empowered by the Holy Spirit, it would be His crucifixion, the empty tomb, and His ascension to heaven that would grip their hearts.

As Jesus lived among them, however, the training they would receive would primarily come through informal "as you go" teaching as opposed to more formal classroom instruction. By the Lord's consistent, day-to-day example, they would bond as intimate friends. Looking more closely, it was not just what was "taught," but it was also what was "caught" that made the learning experience most valuable to the disciples. While the disciples' everyday life with Jesus was quite unique, it was through the sharing of His life on a personal level that He would provide the foundation for the men's ministries that are so desperately needed in our churches today.

With this in mind, I offer this book, not as yet "another" instruction manual on how to perform better for God, or as an absolute pattern for men's ministry, but as a inspiration to connect not only on a deeper level with Christ but in relationship with other Christian brothers (John 15). As these connections happen, Christian men are more likely to find the necessary encouragement to assume their God-given (male) leadership roles in their homes and churches, in the workplace, and in their communities. As men are challenged as a team, they are much more likely to finish well rather than become spiritual casualties.

This book, in part, accounts for my thoughts over three years as I invited a small group of men to join me on a journey with God, asking the Lord to develop a ministry to men on a scale that had not existed before. It is divided into sections, primarily comprised of God's words that were used to promote a biblical vision in our hearts. By making vertical and horizontal relationships a priority, God has transitioned us from mere casual friends to more intimate teammates, united in heart and more focused than ever to make our lives count for Jesus Christ, particularly among those men in our sphere of influence. During the last three years, as we have been more intentional in sharing our lives, we have all been changed in one way or another. Biblical terms such as servant, shepherd/leadership, faith, obedience, and sacrifice have taken on new meaning.

As it was with us, may God give you a fresh "heart"

vision/perspective that would cause you to "Rise to God's Call" as part of a team, perhaps in a leadership role, standing with other men in "the arena" on the "playing field" of life. May you encourage one another to be men of purpose, authenticity, and influence who produce eternal fruit, each in his own way, who bring glory and honor and praise to the name of Jesus Christ.

Larry Garland

"MY HEART IS STIRRED BY A NOBLE THEME"...Psalm 45:1 (NIV)
"Speak, for your servant is listening."
1 Samuel 3:10b (NRSV)

"And the Lord answered me, and said, Write the vision, and make it plain upon tables, that he may run that readeth it. For the vision is yet for an appointed time, but at the end it shall speak, and not lie: though it tarry, wait for it; because it will surely come, it will not tarry."
Habakkuk 2:2-3

"Where there is no vision, the people perish."
Proverbs 29:18a

SECTION 1 – INSPIRATION

Approximately six years ago, the book that you hold in your hands had its beginning through a prayer that went something like this: "God, I don't have as much time left as I had when I was younger…What do you want me to do with the rest of my life?" His answer came as a result of a renewed appreciation for God's grace in my life and His unconditional love for me through Jesus Christ. With this as inspiration, I sensed that God had been preparing me to partner with some other men from my home church to begin a ministry among us whereby we could encourage one another as well as our other Christian brothers in becoming more purposeful in our walk as disciples/servants of Jesus Christ. Along the way, as I began this adventure, there would be visible confirmation that, indeed, this was His idea and not mine. And in obedience to His call, it would become my personal vision, passion, and a joy in my life.

> "…but were eyewitnesses of his majesty. For he received from God the Father honour and glory, when there came such a voice to him from the excellent glory, This is my beloved Son, in whom I am well pleased."
> **2 Peter 1:16-17**

CONNECTING MEN TO MEN THROUGH CHRIST

The Big Picture Vision

The Promotion of:

A **Passion** for Worshiping God
"…Thou shalt love the Lord thy God with all thy heart, and with all thy soul, and with all thy mind."
Matthew 22:37

A **Passion** for Connecting Men
"…so that we may be mutually encouraged by each other's faith, both yours and mine."
Romans 1:12 (NRSV)

A **Passion** for Building Up Believers
"For the perfecting of the saints, for the work of the ministry, for the edifying of the body of Christ: Till we all come in the unity of the faith, and of the knowledge of the Son of God, unto a perfect man, unto the measure of the stature of the fulness of Christ."
Ephesians 4:12-13

A **Passion** for Reaching Non-Believers
"Then saith he unto his disciples, The harvest truly is plenteous, but the labourers are few; Pray ye therefore the Lord of the harvest, that he will send forth labourers into his harvest."
Matthew 9:37-38

For the Advancement of God's Kingdom and Glory
"After this manner, therefore, pray ye: Our Father which art in heaven, Hallowed be thy name. Thy kingdom come. Thy will be done in earth, as it is in heaven."
Matthew 6:9-10

CONNECTING MEN TO MEN THROUGH CHRIST

The Vision of Men's Ministry

The Purpose

A ministry that is committed to the building of a network of men that emphasizes deeper personal relationships, encourages discipleship training, equips, and energizes each man to realize his potential in Christ and grow to maturity, using his natural and spiritual gifts to impact lives at home, in the church, and in the community for the advancement of the gospel and the glory of God.

The Prayer

"Now the God of peace, that brought again from the dead our Lord Jesus, that great Shepherd of the sheep, through the blood of the everlasting covenant, make you perfect in every good work to do his will, working in you that which is well pleasing in his sight, through Jesus Christ, to whom be glory forever and ever. Amen."
Hebrews 13:20-21

CONNECTING MEN TO MEN THROUGH CHRIST

Embracing the Vision

"And I sought for a man among them, that should make up the hedge, and stand in the gap before me for the land, that I should not destroy it: but I found none."
Ezekiel 22:30

> "God's plan is to make much of the man, far more of him than anything else, because men are God's method. The church is looking for better methods; God is looking for better men. The Holy Ghost does not flow through methods but through men. He does not come on machines, but on men. He does not anoint plans but men. It is not great talents nor great learning that God needs, but men great in holiness, great in faith, great in love, great in fidelity, great for God. Those men can mold a generation for God."
> **E.M. Bounds,** *The Power of Prayer*

"And he said, Go forth, and stand upon the mount before the LORD. And, behold, the LORD passed by, and a great and strong wind rent the mountains, and brake in pieces the rocks before the LORD; but the LORD was not in the wind: and after the wind an earthquake; but the LORD was not in the earthquake: And after the earthquake a fire; but the LORD was not in the fire: and after the fire a still small voice."
1 Kings 19:11-12

CONNECTING MEN TO MEN THROUGH CHRIST

Expanding the Vision

"Only let your conduct be worthy the gospel of Christ, so that whether I come and see you or am absent, I may here of your affairs, that you may stand fast in one spirit, with one mind striving together for the faith of the gospel."
Philippians 1:27 (NKJV)

— VISION PARTNERS —

As part of the mission and vision of Jesus Christ for his church, the desire would be for the Connecting Men to Men ministry to grow to include the building of relationships with men from other area churches so that there might be mutual encouragement from the challenge of Matthew 28:18-20 (the Great Commission) and 2 Timothy 2:2.

"IF YOUR PARTNER IS GOD,
MAKE YOUR PLANS BIG!"
D.L. Moody

SECTION 2 – INVITATION

Following my convictions, the next step was to begin praying for God's timing and wisdom regarding those men He was preparing to join me in making His vision for the men of our local church a reality. Eventually, after approximately three years of reading, thinking, and praying, I invited seven men to "leave their nets," so to speak, and after a time of training, begin using our various gifts to disciple men in obedience to the "Great Commission" of Matthew 28:18-20. Using a series of DVDs by John Eldredge entitled *Wild at Heart* to generate discussion at our bimonthly gatherings, a common thread that became apparent was both our desire and our need as Christian brothers to accept this challenge to fight for the hearts and lives of other men. After three years, and despite our many differences, the call for us to disciple men for Christ as a team, each man in his own way, continues to be a mutual commitment that has provided great personal peace and satisfaction.

> "And he saith unto them, Follow me, and I will make you fishers of men. And they straightway left their nets, and followed him."
> **Matthew 4:19-20**

Connecting Men to Men Through Christ

It Begins With a Small Group of Men

A Core group is formed:

- Hearts are developed using a catalyst for fellowship, like the John Eldredge DVD
- Trusting relationships are established
- The men become a team with commitment to each other and the gospel
- There is validation and affirmation

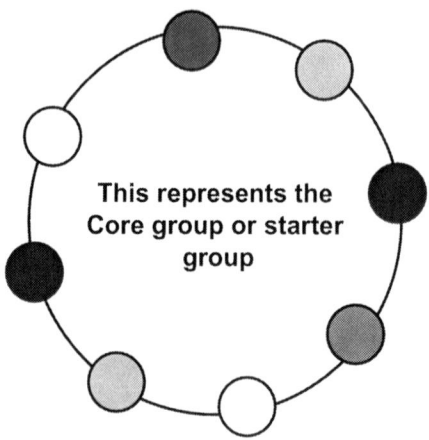

This represents the Core group or starter group

The men's group satisfies the ministry vision of pursuing a passion for God as individuals and as a group:

- Personal living
- Prioritizing eternal values
- Active participation
- Building intentional biblical relationships
- Caring for each other's spiritual and emotional needs
- Discovering gifts
- Partnering and encouragement

Connecting as Companions

"The rule of synergy is that you are supposed to accomplish more together than your combined individual output could produce."*

Therefore

"Part of our role should be to affirm God's call on the lives of our companions and to do everything we can to ensure their success and obedience to God's assignments."*

"Paul watched for young men in whom he could invest and whom he could encourage in the faith."*

"For as we have many members in one body, and all members have not the same office: So we, being many, are one body in Christ, and every one members one of another. Having then gifts differing according to the grace that is given to us..."
Romans 12:4-6

**Anointed to be God's Servants,*
by Henry & Tom Blackaby

CONNECTING MEN TO MEN THROUGH CHRIST

Understanding the Mission

"And Jesus came and said to them, 'All authority in heaven and on earth has been given to me. Go therefore and make disciples of all nations, baptizing them in the name of the Father and of the Son and of the Holy Spirit, and teaching them to obey everything that I have commanded you. And remember, I am with you always, to the end of the age.'"
Matthew 28:18-20 (NRSV)

"We succeed only as we identify in life, or in war, or in anything else, a single overriding objective, and make all other considerations bend to that one objective."
Dwight D. Eisenhower

Go and Make Disciples!

Giving God the Glory!

CONNECTING MEN TO MEN THROUGH CHRIST

A Matter of Prayer

"Trust in the Lord with all thine heart; and lean not unto thine own understanding. In all thy ways acknowledge him, and he shall direct thy paths."
Proverbs 3:5-6

"We are bound to thank God always for you, brethren, as it is fitting, because your faith grows exceedingly, and the love of every one of you all abounds toward each other...Therefore we also pray always for you that our God would count you worthy of this calling, and fulfill all the good pleasure of His goodness and the work of faith with power, that the name of our Lord Jesus Christ may be glorified in you, and you in Him, according to the grace of our God and the Lord Jesus Christ."
2 Thessalonians 1:3,11-12 (NKJV)

"Call to Me, and I will answer you, and show you great and mighty things, which you do not know."
Jeremiah 33:3 (NKJV)

SECTION 3 – INFORMATION

From the very beginning of our first year together, as a team of eight, I sensed that the challenge of connecting the men so as to get them all on the same page would not be an easy task. It wasn't much comfort to be aware that I had no clear game plan for a men's ministry in completed form, but I knew God would be faithful if I was obedient. All I needed to do was to keep my heart focused on Christ, make prayer a priority, and keep the men focused on the character of God and the word of God. As we continued to view the series of DVDs by John Eldredge to stimulate our discussions, they proved invaluable in uniting our hearts. Together, we set our hearts on the race before us, asking for the knowledge and depth of insight necessary for us to stay on target. As the weeks and months passed, we were all beginning to sense that God had plans in mind that He would reveal to us in His way and in His time and, as a team, we wanted to be part of them.

> "And this I pray, that your love may abound yet more and more in knowledge and in all judgment; That ye may approve things that are excellent; that ye may be sincere and without offence till the day of Christ"
> **Philippians 1:9-10**

CONNECTING MEN TO MEN THROUGH CHRIST

Setting Their Hearts

"For surely I know the plans I have for you, says the Lord, plans for your welfare and not for harm, to give you a future with hope. Then when you call upon me and come and pray to me, I will hear you. When you search for me, you will find me; if you seek me with all your heart..."
Jeremiah 29:11-13 (NRSV)

"But when he saw the multitudes, he was moved with compassion on them...

"If anyone sets his heart on being an overseer, he desires a noble task."
1 Timothy 3:1 (NIV)

...because they fainted, and were scattered abroad, as sheep having no shepherd."
Matt. 9:36

"He who believes in Me, as the Scripture has said, out of his heart will flow rivers of living water."
John 7:38 (NKJV)

"My passion is to multiply all that God has given me, and in the process, give it back."
Bob Buford, *Halftime*

CONNECTING MEN TO MEN THROUGH CHRIST

Running the Race

"That ye may be blameless and harmless, the sons of God, without rebuke, in the midst of a crooked and perverse nation, among whom ye shine as lights in the world; Holding forth the word of life..."
Philippians 2:15-16a

PASSION
"Know ye not that they which run in a race run all, but one receiveth the prize?
1 Cor. 9:24

"Not by might nor by power, but by my Spirit."
Zechariah 4:6

PURPOSE
"I therefore so run, not as uncertainly; so fight I, not as one that beateth the air..."
1 Cor. 9:26

"...let us lay aside every weight, and the sin which doth so easily beset us, and let us run with patience the race that is set before us, Looking unto Jesus the author and finisher of our faith..."
Hebrews 12:1b-2a

"Life is no brief candle to me. It's a sort of splendid torch which I've got hold of for the moment, and I want to make it burn as brightly as possible before handing it on to future generations."
George Bernard Shaw

CONNECTING MEN TO MEN THROUGH CHRIST

Passing the Baton

"Thou therefore, my son, be strong in the grace that is in Christ Jesus. And the things that thou hast heard of me among many witnesses, the same commit thou to faithful men, who shall be able to teach others also."
2 Timothy 2:1-2

Inspiration and Aspiration

> "Your young men will see visions; your old men will dream dreams."
> **Acts 2:17b**

Duplication and Multiplication

"One generation shall praise thy works to another, and shall declare thy mighty acts. I will speak of the glorious honour of thy majesty, and of thy wondrous works. And men shall speak of the might of thy terrible [awe-inspiring] acts: and I will declare thy greatness."
Psalm 145:4-6

> "You can influence a man from a distance, but you impact him up close."
> **Howard Hendricks**

CONNECTING MEN TO MEN THROUGH CHRIST

Staying on Target

"... REMEMBER MY CHAINS ..."
Colossians 4:18 (NKJV)

" I eagerly expect and hope that I will in no way be ashamed, but will have sufficient courage so that now as always Christ will be exalted in my body, whether by life or by death. For to me, to live is Christ and to die is gain. If I am to go on living in the body, this will mean fruitful labor for me. Yet what shall I choose? I do not know! I am torn between the two: I desire to depart and be with Christ, which is better by far; but it is more necessary for you that I remain in the body. Convinced of this, I know that I will remain, and I will continue with all of you for your progress and joy in the faith, so that through my being with you again your joy in Christ Jesus will overflow on account of me."
Philippians 1:20-21, 25-26 (NIV)

"The archer's aim must be sure, for he who overshoots his mark does no better than he who falls short of it."

Author Unknown

SECTION 4 - INTEGRATION

Gradually, as our time spent together increased, our depth of friendship with each other and, most importantly, with the Lord Jesus was on the increase as well. Our concern for one another and our commitment to what He wanted to do in and through us to bring glory to the Father was, indeed, changing. As we shared and searched the scriptures together, we were challenged as individual members of a team to build greater balance and discipline into our lives, with Jesus alone as the centerpiece of our efforts. In our discussions, we focused on topics such as character, conversation, conduct, and stewardship. With personal accountability as our priority, I sensed we were making both individual as well as team progress, one step at a time. In the words of John Eldredge, our vision was truly becoming all about the heartfelt challenge of "Deep Friendships and a Shared Mission," encouraging other men to reach their potential as servants of Jesus Christ.

> "…work out your own salvation with fear and trembling. For it is God which worketh in you both to will and to do of his good pleasure."
> **Philippians 2:12b-13**

CONNECTING MEN TO MEN THROUGH CHRIST

Balancing Their Lives

"I am crucified with Christ: nevertheless I live; yet not I, but Christ liveth in me: and the life which I now live in the flesh I live by the faith of the Son of God, who loved me, and gave himself for me."
Galatians 2:20

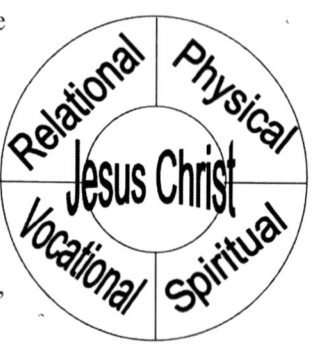

"If ye then, be risen with Christ, seek those things which are above, where Christ sitteth on the right hand of God."
Col. 3:1

"Set your affection on things above, not on things on the earth. For ye are dead, and your life is hid with Christ in God."
Col. 3:2-3

"Don't seek a ministry, but expect the fruit of a well-disciplined life."
Bill Gothard

CONNECTING MEN TO MEN THROUGH CHRIST

Raising the Standard

"For the love of Christ constraineth us; because we thus judge, that if one died for all, then were all dead: And that he died for all, that they which live should not henceforth live unto themselves, but unto him which died for them, and rose again."
2 Corinthians 5:14-15

Character – Who I Am!
1 Timothy 4:12b

Conversation – What I Say!
Colossians 4:6

Conduct – How I Live!
Jeremiah 17:10

Converts – What God Does!
Ephesians 2:8-10

"Herein is my Father glorified, that ye bear much fruit; so shall ye be my disciples."
John 15:8

CONNECTING MEN TO MEN THROUGH CHRIST

Growing in Grace

"But grow in grace, and in the knowledge of our Lord and Saviour Jesus Christ. To him be glory both now and for ever. Amen."
2 Peter 3:18

> "As I look back now on the task our Lord was seeking to accomplish in us, I stand in awe in both what he did and how he did it. Before his departure he would make certain he had equipped us with all the knowledge and tools we would need to continue the movement that would ultimately impact the entire world. Yet with so little time and so much to be done, all he asked of us was our willingness to build a friendship with him. He simply invited us to stay by his side, to eat with him, to walk with him, to camp out with him, to listen to him, to learn from his example, to build a comradeship with God in human form. Jesus did not attempt to bring us to a point of competency in knowledge or techniques or programs. He simply sought to draw us into a depth of friendship with himself, a friendship that would ultimately become the driving motivation in every aspect of our lives."
>
> **Larry Huntsperger,** *The Fisherman*

"In the beginning was the Word, and the Word was with God, and the Word was God...And the Word was made flesh, and dwelt among us, (and we beheld his glory, the glory as of the only begotten of the Father,) full of grace and truth."
John 1:1,14

CONNECTING MEN TO MEN THROUGH CHRIST

Proving Their Faith

"Let a man so account of us, as of the ministers of Christ, and stewards of the mysteries of God. Moreover it is required in stewards, that a man be found faithful."
1 Corinthians 4:1-2

Time

Treasure

Talent

Testimony

"But you know that Timothy has proved himself, because as a son with his father he has served with me in the work of the gospel."
Philippians 2:22 (NIV)

"The greatest thought that has ever entered my mind is that one day I will have to stand before a holy God and give an account of my life."
Daniel Webster

CONNECTING MEN TO MEN THROUGH CHRIST

Progressing in Ministry

Premise
Deep Friendships and a Shared Mission
"I no longer call you servants…Instead, I have called you friends…go and bear fruit—fruit that will last."
John 15:15-16

Price
"And he said to them all, If any man will come after me, let him deny himself, and take up his cross daily, and follow me."
Luke 9:23

"And Jesus said unto him, No man, having put his hand to the plough, and looking back, is fit for the kingdom of God."
Luke 9:62

Perception
- **Endure** as a soldier
- **Train** as an athlete
- **Work** hard as a farmer

2 Tim. 2:3-6

Promise
"The one who calls you is faithful and he will do it."
1 Thessalonians 5:24 (NIV)

Praise
"… the joy of the Lord is our strength."
Nehemiah 8:10b

"…They will be called oaks of righteousness, the planting of the Lord, to display his glory."
Isaiah 61:3 (NRSV)

SECTION 5 – IDENTIFICATION

Encouraged by what God was doing among us in terms of unity and team spirit, our next step was to have an event whereby our current vision/game plan could be shared with the rest of our church brothers for the purpose of generating more interest. God was pleased to raise up seven additional men to join us in our journey. Because we already had some direction as to how He wanted us to proceed, it wasn't long before our new teammates had a good sense of what we were about. As we were growing in numbers, it became important and necessary to begin sharing the workload in order to be most effective. Consequently, the time had come to identify and select those men from the team who were best equipped to be "out front" leaders as well as those who were better suited for support roles as allies. For some of the men, the faith decision to "get out of the boat" would come sooner than they expected, but it would prove to be a decision they would not regret.

> "But select capable men from all the people—men who fear God, trustworthy men who hate dishonest gain—and appoint them as officials over thousands, hundreds, fifties and tens...That will make your load lighter, because they will share it with you."
> **Exodus 18:21, 22b (NIV)**

CONNECTING MEN TO MEN THROUGH CHRIST

Continuing the Vision

"But continue thou in the things which thou hast learned and hast been assured of, knowing of whom thou hast learned them."
2 Timothy 3:14

Create Leadership
Exodus 18:18-22

Cultivate Allies
1 Chronicles 11:10

Communicate Openly
Proverbs 25:11

Celebrate Joyfully
Psalm 145:1-7

"...but to wait for the Promise of the Father, "which," He said, "you have heard from Me."...But you shall receive power when the Holy Spirit has come upon you; and you shall be witnesses to Me in Jerusalem, and in all Judea and Samaria, and to the end of the earth."
Acts 1:4b,8 (NKJV)

CONNECTING MEN TO MEN THROUGH CHRIST

Laying the Foundation

"For other foundation can no man lay than that is laid, which is Jesus Christ."
1 Corinthians 3:11

Character
1 Corinthians 4:17b

Unity
John 17:20-21

Courage
Acts 4:13

Perseverance
Galatians 6:7-9

"So then neither is he that planteth any thing, neither he that watereth; but God that giveth the increase."
1 Corinthians 3:7

CONNECTING MEN TO MEN THROUGH CHRIST

Shepherd/Leader Oversight

"Therefore take heed to yourselves and to all the flock, among which the Holy Spirit has made you overseers..."
Acts 20:28 (NKJV)

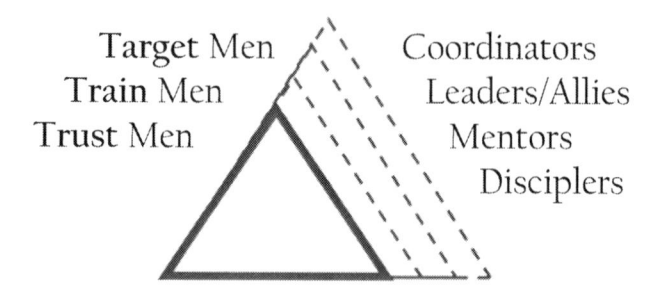

Target Men — Coordinators
Train Men — Leaders/Allies
Trust Men — Mentors
— Disciplers

The strength of the pyramid is determined by the breadth of its base!
From "Cell Ministry Training"

CONNECTING MEN TO MEN THROUGH CHRIST

Relationship Development
Don't live in too small of an adventure with God!

"Now when Jesus came into the district of Caesarea Philippi, he asked his disciples, 'Who do people say that the Son of Man is?'...Simon Peter answered, 'You are the Messiah, the Son of the living God.' And Jesus answered, 'Blessed are you, Simon son of Jonah! For flesh and blood has not revealed this to you, but my Father in heaven. And I tell you, you are Peter, and on this rock I will build my church, and the gates of Hades will not prevail against it.'"
Matthew 16:13, 16-18 (NRSV)

"Six days later, Jesus took with him Peter and James and his brother John and led them up a high mountain, by themselves. And he was transfigured before them, and his face shone like the sun, and his clothes became dazzling white...While he was still speaking, suddenly a bright cloud overshadowed them, and from the cloud a voice said, 'This is my Son, the Beloved; with him I am well pleased; listen to him! When the disciples heard this, they fell to the ground and were overcome by fear. But Jesus came and touched them, saying, 'Get up and do not be afraid.' And when they looked up, they saw no one except Jesus himself alone.'"
Matthew 17:1-2, 5-8 (NRSV)

"He said to him the third time, 'Simon son of John, do you love me?' Peter felt hurt because he said to him the third time, 'Do you love me?' And he said to him, 'Lord, you know everything; you know that I love you.' Jesus said to him, 'Feed my sheep.'"
John 21:17 (NRSV)

"Find out where God is working, and join him there."
Henry Blackaby, *Experiencing God*

CONNECTING MEN TO MEN THROUGH CHRIST

Taking the Initiative

"He said, 'Come.' So Peter got out of the boat, started walking on the water, and came toward Jesus."
Matthew 14:29 (NRSV)

"My life was comfortable but I longed for something. I wanted to make a difference."
John Ortberg

"When they saw the courage of Peter and John and realized that they were unschooled, ordinary men, they were astonished and they took note that these men had been with Jesus."
Acts 4:13 (NIV)

"The decision to grow always involves a choice between risk and comfort."
John Ortberg

"Two roads diverged in a wood, and I—I took the one less traveled by. And that has made all the difference."
Robert Frost

SECTION 6 – INTERDEPENDENCE

Again, the time had come for God to assign each of us new roles so His plans could move forward according to His schedule. I remember being both appreciative and amazed of what God had accomplished in us thus far. In just over a year and a half, He had assembled a very diverse group of men, much like He did with the twelve original disciples. After a time of training and personal growth with Jesus, they would go forth as faithful witnesses to the truth of the gospel message. The love, acceptance, and sense of purpose that they received as they lived with Jesus, so many years ago, was fast becoming the model for us to emulate. Somehow, despite our individual differences in age, giftedness, maturity level, and stage of life, we had been prepared to function as a team for the glory of a God who could and would do "things beyond our understanding" in and through us if we would only let him. The sense of community that we were experiencing had become part of that "something more" we had needed in our lives as Christian men for so long, and we wanted it to show.

> "But God composed the body, having given greater honor to that part which lacks it, that there should be no schism in the body, but that the members should have the same care for one another."
> **1 Corinthians 12:24b-25 (NKJV)**

CONNECTING MEN TO MEN THROUGH CHRIST

Setting the Pace

"Be ye followers of me, even as I also am of Christ."
1 Corinthians 11:1

"A disciple is not above the teacher, but everyone who is fully qualified will be like the teacher."
Luke 6:40 (NRSV)

Giftedness
2 Timothy 1:6

Maturity
Hebrews 5:14

Passion
Acts 20:24

Availability
Isaiah 6:8

Stage of Life Factor
Survival ● Success ● Significance

"…be strong, therefore, and prove yourself a man. And keep the charge of the Lord your God: to walk in His ways…that you may prosper in all that you do and wherever you turn."
1 Kings 2:2b-3 (NKJV)

CONNECTING MEN TO MEN THROUGH CHRIST

Experiencing Their Giftedness

> "What lies behind us and what lies before us are small matters compared to what lies within us."
> **Ralph Waldo Emerson**

"Greatly desiring to see thee, being mindful of thy tears, that I may be filled with joy…Wherefore I put thee in remembrance that thou stir up the gift of God, which is in thee by the putting on of my hands. For God hath not given us the spirit of fear; but of power, and of love, and of a sound mind. Be not thou therefore ashamed of the testimony of our Lord, nor of me his prisoner: but be thou partaker of the afflictions of the gospel according to the power of God; Who hath saved us, and called us with an holy calling, not according to our works, but according to his own purpose and grace, which was given us in Christ Jesus before the world began..."
2 Timothy 1:4, 6-9

> "The reason most people do not see Jordan Rivers parting in their lives and ministries is because they waver at the riverbank."
> **Henry & Richard Blackaby,**
> *Called to be God's Leader*

CONNECTING MEN TO MEN THROUGH CHRIST

Leading by Example

"If I then, your Lord and Master, have washed your feet; ye also ought to wash one another's feet. For I have given you an example, that ye should do as I have done to you. Verily, verily, I say unto you, The servant is not greater than his lord; neither he that is sent greater than he that sent him."
John 13:14-16

"I'd rather see a sermon than hear one any day; I'd rather one should walk with me than merely tell the way. The eye's a better pupil and more willing than the ear, Fine counsel is confusing, but example's always clear; And the best of all preachers are the men who live their creeds, For to see good put in action is what everybody needs...And the lecture you deliver may be very wise and true, But I'd rather get my lessons by observing what you do; For I might misunderstand you and the high advice you give, But there's no misunderstanding how you act and how you live...Though an able speaker charms me with his eloquence, I say, I'd rather see a sermon than to hear one, any day."

Edgar A. Guest, *Sermons We See*

"A new commandment I give unto you, That ye love one another; as I have loved you, that ye also love one another. By this shall all men know that ye are my disciples, if ye have love one to another."
John 13:34-35

CONNECTING MEN TO MEN THROUGH CHRIST

Realizing Their Potential

"But now, O Lord, thou art our father;
we are the clay, and thou our potter;
and we all are the work of thy hand."
Isaiah 64:8

"Now faith is the substance of things hoped for...

"Keep alert, stand firm in your faith, be courageous, be strong."
1 Cor. 16:13 (NRSV)

...the evidence of things not seen."
Heb. 11:1

"But as we were allowed of God to be put in trust with the gospel, even so we speak; not as pleasing men, but God, which trieth our hearts."
1 Thessalonians 2:4

"Now unto him that is able to do exceeding abundantly above all that we ask or think, according to the power that worketh in us, Unto him be glory in the church by Christ Jesus throughout all ages, world without end. Amen."
Ephesians 3:20-21

SECTION 7 – IMPLEMENTATION

As God was communicating the changes He needed to make, the next step for the growth of the ministry was to provide what are now referred to as "environments for investment!" Specifically, these would be opportunities for men to connect in a variety of planned activities for the purpose of relationship development. It was important to offer enough options so that all the men of the church could plug in at their particular interest and comfort level. Although many of the activities would be more casual and informal, while others would have a little more structure, all would be geared toward building friendships that should grow and deepen over time. Periodically, special larger events would be planned, with men of godly character and influence asked to encourage the men to a more purposeful relationship with Jesus Christ. We would continue to make prayer a priority, asking God to work in our hearts in such a way as it would please Him so that He would receive the greatest possible glory.

> "Commit thy works unto the Lord, and thy thoughts shall be established. A man's heart deviseth his way: but the Lord directeth his steps."
> **Proverbs 16:3, 9**

CONNECTING MEN TO MEN THROUGH CHRIST

Following a Plan

> "And let us consider how we may spur one another on toward love and good deeds."
> **Hebrews 10:24 (NIV)**
>
> "...that we may present every man perfect in Christ Jesus."
> **Colossians 1:28b**

Fellowship Groups

Social activities and events that provide opportunity for relaxation, refreshment, and relationships that promote team vision, unity, and spirit.

Focus Groups

An informal time of Bible instruction and discussion on a variety of topics where relationship development with God and other men becomes a priority as part of a Christ-centered lifestyle.

Friendship Groups

Special relationships that grow, deepen, and become more personal over time due to chemistry, trust, and common interests.

Faith Partner(s)

A mentoring/discipleship relationship between two or three men that enables them to encourage each other to maximize their potential in Jesus Christ.

Field Service Groups

Opportunity for men to work together, using their natural gifts and practical skills in various service projects, to meet needs within the church as well as in the community as servants of Jesus Christ.

CONNECTING MEN TO MEN THROUGH CHRIST

Environments for Investment

"But he that received seed into the good ground is he that heareth the word, and understandeth it; which also beareth fruit, and bringeth forth, some an hundredfold, some sixty, some thirty."
Matthew 13:23

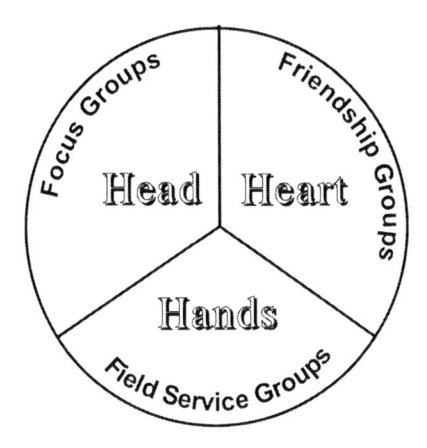

[Diagram: A circle divided into three sections labeled "Head", "Heart", and "Hands", with outer labels "Focus Groups", "Friendship Groups", and "Field Service Groups".]

"Two are better than one; because they have a good reward for their labour. For if they fall, the one will lift up his fellow: but woe to him that is alone when he falleth; for he hath not another to help him up...For if they fall, the one will lift up his fellow: but woe to him that is alone when he falleth; for he hath not another to help him up."
Ecclesiastes 4:9,10,12a

"Fruit cannot be manufactured. Fruit grows on its own in the right circumstances and given a suitable environment."

John MacArthur

CONNECTING MEN TO MEN THROUGH CHRIST

THE HUDDLE

A periodic event—held for the purpose of creating an environment for fellowship and relationship building among the men and their guests—that promotes unity, team spirit, and a lifestyle that honors Jesus Christ and brings glory to God.

"How good and pleasant it is
when brothers live together in unity!"
Psalm 133:1 (NIV)

CONNECTING MEN TO MEN THROUGH CHRIST

THE SUMMIT

An annual weekend event that takes place in a retreat setting. All men ages 16 and up are invited for a relaxing time of fellowship in a Christ-centered environment to "get away from it all," so to speak. A variety of activities are offered where the men can compete together or simply enjoy moments where new friendships are made, as well as existing ones deepened. As always, this unhurried atmosphere proves to be a great time of spiritual refreshment and challenge.

"A generous man will prosper; he who refreshes others will himself be refreshed."
Proverbs 11:25 (NIV)

CONNECTING MEN TO MEN THROUGH CHRIST

Connecting in Focus Groups

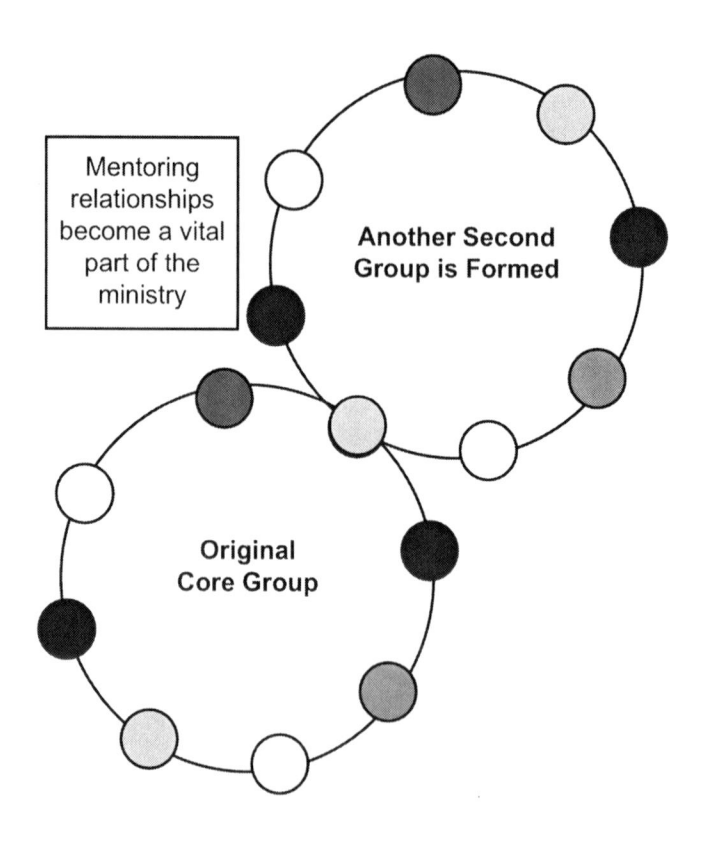

Mentoring relationships become a vital part of the ministry

Another Second Group is Formed

Original Core Group

SECTION 8 – INTERACTION

Toward the end of our second year, we introduced home "Focus Groups" as one of the primary options for the men to connect, providing them with greater opportunity to share more of their lives together. As anticipated, these gatherings proved to be much more than mere meetings for the purpose of accumulating an excessive amount of information or knowledge without practical application. Commenting on their experience, many of the men sensed that they were becoming more like encouragers and servants of one another just as Jesus had commanded His first small group of disciples. A network of men—on the same page, committed to Jesus and to one another, and for all the right reasons—was slowly becoming a reality. God's plans were surfacing, the men were growing, and the journey was becoming more exciting all the time.

> "We loved you so much that we were delighted to share with you not only the gospel of God but our lives as well, because you had become so dear to us."
> **1 Thessalonians 2:8 (NIV)**

CONNECTING MEN TO MEN THROUGH CHRIST

Instruction and Discussion

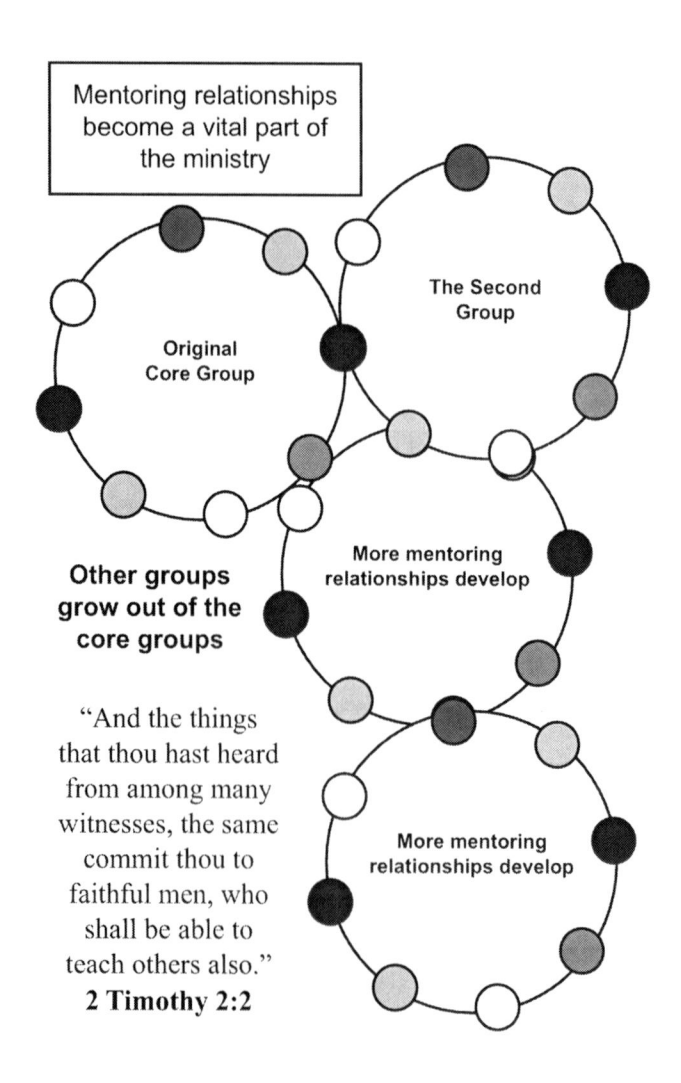

Mentoring relationships become a vital part of the ministry

Original Core Group

The Second Group

More mentoring relationships develop

More mentoring relationships develop

Other groups grow out of the core groups

"And the things that thou hast heard from among many witnesses, the same commit thou to faithful men, who shall be able to teach others also."
2 Timothy 2:2

CONNECTING MEN TO MEN THROUGH CHRIST

Acceptance and Encouragement

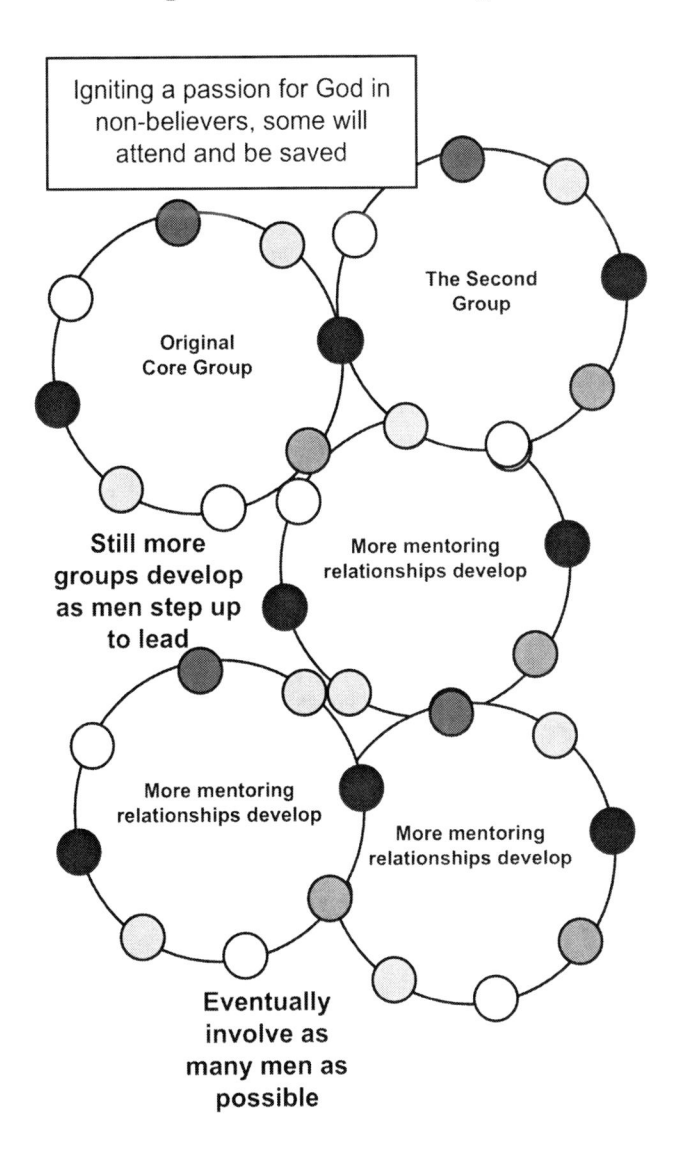

Igniting a passion for God in non-believers, some will attend and be saved

Original Core Group

The Second Group

Still more groups develop as men step up to lead

More mentoring relationships develop

More mentoring relationships develop

More mentoring relationships develop

Eventually involve as many men as possible

61

CONNECTING MEN TO MEN THROUGH CHRIST

Christ-Centered Lifestyles

"As ye have therefore received Christ Jesus the Lord, so walk ye in him: Rooted and built up in him, and stablished in the faith, as ye have been taught, abounding therein with thanksgiving."
Colossians 2:6-7

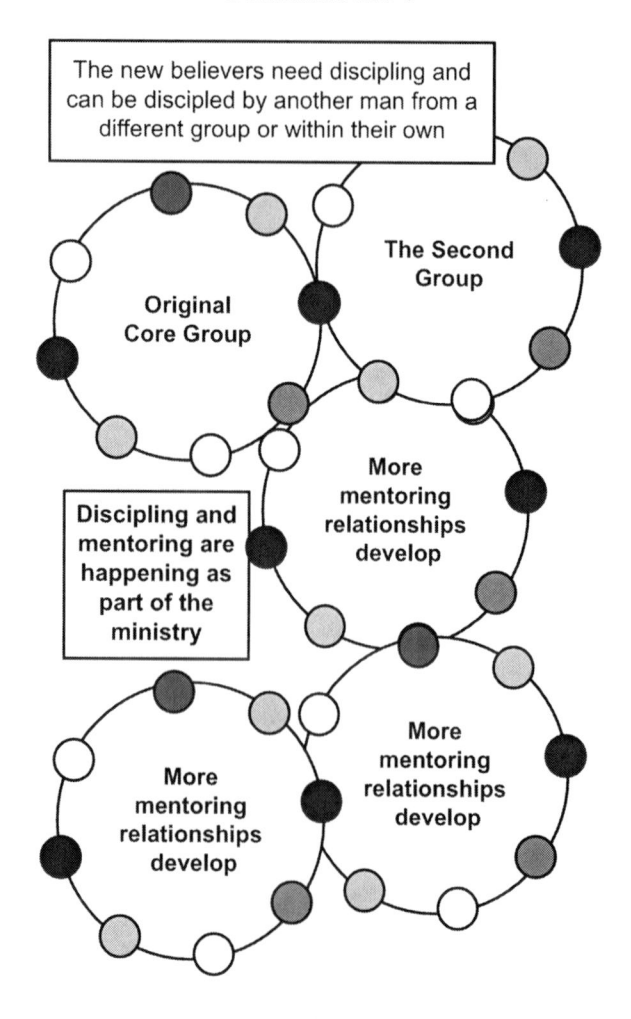

The new believers need discipling and can be discipled by another man from a different group or within their own

Original Core Group

The Second Group

Discipling and mentoring are happening as part of the ministry

More mentoring relationships develop

More mentoring relationships develop

More mentoring relationships develop

CONNECTING MEN TO MEN THROUGH CHRIST

Sharing Their Stories

"For by grace are ye saved through faith; and that not of yourselves: it is the gift of God: Not of works, lest any man should boast. For we are his workmanship, created in Christ Jesus unto good works, which God hath before ordained that we should walk in them."
Ephesians 2:8-10

Remember
2 Timothy 1:12-14

Reflect
Romans 7:21-25

Resolve
Hebrews 4:14-16

"I am not what I hoped I would be. Nor am I what I want to be. But by the GRACE OF GOD, I'm not what I used to be. I once was lost, but now I'm found, was blind, but now I see."
Charlie "Tremendous" Jones

CONNECTING MEN TO MEN THROUGH CHRIST

Building Friendships

"A friend loveth at all times,
and a brother is born for adversity."
Proverbs 17:17

Listen to your brother with your heart.

Empathize with your brother's struggles and burdens.

Ask your brother questions that will provide greater understanding.

Direct your brother to the character and heart of God through the word of God.

> "A friend is one who knows you as you are, understands where you've been, accepts who you've become, and still invites you to grow."
> **Stu Weber,** *Locking Arms*

CONNECTING MEN TO MEN THROUGH CHRIST

Prioritizing God's Word

"For ever, O Lord, thy word is settled in heaven...Thy testimonies have I taken as an heritage forever: for they are the rejoicing of my heart."
Psalm 119:89,111

"Blessed is the man that walketh not in the counsel of the ungodly, nor standeth in the way of sinners, nor sitteth in the seat of the scornful. But his delight is in the law of the Lord; and in his law doth he meditate day and night. And he shall be like a tree planted by the rivers of water, that bringeth forth his fruit in his season; his leaf also shall not wither; and whatsoever he doeth shall prosper. "
Psalm 1:1-3

"Sanctify them through thy truth: thy word is truth."
John 17:17

"Study to shew thyself approved unto God, a workman that needeth not to be ashamed, rightly dividing the word of truth."
2 Timothy 2:15

CONNECTING MEN TO MEN THROUGH CHRIST

Growing in the Process

"Teach the older men to be temperate, worthy of respect, self-controlled, and sound in faith, in love and in endurance."
Titus 2:2 (NIV)

Grow the Man

"We are bound to thank God always for you, brethren, as it is meet, because that your faith groweth exceedingly, and the charity of every one of you all toward each other aboundeth"
2 Thessalonians 1:3

Grow the Church

"From whom the whole body fitly joined together and compacted by that which every joint supplieth, according to the effectual working in the measure of every part, maketh increase of the body unto the edifying of itself in love."
Ephesians 4:16

Grow the Kingdom

"And they continued stedfastly in the apostles' doctrine and fellowship, and in breaking of bread, and in prayers...Praising God, and having favour with all the people. And the Lord added to the church daily such as should be saved."
Acts 2:42,47

"Similarly, encourage the young men to be self-controlled. In everything set them an example by doing what is good."
Titus 2:6-7a (NIV)

SECTION 9 - INVESTMENT

The scope of the vision/game plan was rapidly changing and as we were transitioning from our third year to the fourth, the challenge to invest in the eternal versus the temporary became the predominant theme of the ministry. Following the plans that we had agreed upon, the next thing on the agenda was to shift the emphasis from the group dynamic to include one-on-one mentoring/discipleship relationships. We viewed this as being obedient to the teaching of 2 Timothy 2:2, where Paul encouraged his young student and companion, Timothy—investing in him so that he would go on to train other men who would then be qualified to train others. Therefore, an event would be scheduled for later that year called "The Locker Room," where important information would be shared and men's hearts would be prepared, causing them to prayerfully consider whether a "Faith Partner" relationship was right for them at this time.

> "Do not neglect the gift that is in you, which was given to you through prophecy with the laying on of hands by the council of elders. Put these things into practice, devote yourself to them, so that all may see your progress. Pay close attention to yourself and to your teaching; continue in these things, for in doing this you will save both yourself and your hearers."
> **1 Timothy 4:14-16 (NRSV)**

CONNECTING MEN TO MEN THROUGH CHRIST

Refocusing the Vision

The Lord is my shepherd; I shall not want.
He maketh me to lie down in green pastures: he leadeth me beside the still waters.
He restoreth my soul: he leadeth me in the paths of righteousness for his name's sake.
Psalm 23:1-3

"I want to encourage older Christians to believe they have something wonderful to give that only years can supply…If, however, the connection goes beyond acceptance to include penetrating wisdom and spiritual discernment, then friendship has deepened into shepherding."
Dr. Larry Crabb, *Biblical Mandates & Models*

"…and the sheep hear his voice: and he calleth his own sheep by name, and leadeth them out. And when he putteth forth his own sheep, he goeth before them, and the sheep follow him: for they know his voice."
John 10:3b,4

CONNECTING MEN TO MEN THROUGH CHRIST

The Locker Room

"As iron sharpens iron, so one man sharpens another."
Proverbs 27:17 (NIV)

An environment designed to encourage both younger and older men to consider one-on-one mentoring/discipleship relationships as necessary and important for their personal growth as disciples of Jesus Christ. It is anticipated, as men interact in these "faith partner" relationships, that individual strengths will be discovered and developed, as well as weaknesses understood and overcome, resulting in greater competency and confidence for both parties in their God-given roles as men. Also, along the way, the plan is to include ongoing leadership training as an integral part of the agenda.

"Ye are witnesses, and God also, how holily and justly and unblameably we behaved ourselves among you that believe: As ye know how we exhorted and comforted and charged every one of you, as a father doth his children, That ye would walk worthy of God, who hath called you unto his kingdom and glory."
1 Thessalonians 2:10-12

CONNECTING MEN TO MEN THROUGH CHRIST

Finding Their Roles

"Be kindly affectioned one to another with brotherly love; in honour preferring one another; Not slothful in business; fervent in spirit; serving the Lord."
Romans 12:10-11

	Paul "teacher"	
AS LEADERS	Barnabas "encourager"	AS ALLIES
	Timothy "student"	

"If we are to become a generation of mentors and have a culture filled with men of character and wisdom, men that can lead the next generation into true godliness, then we must give careful thought to what men will look like when Christ is formed in them."
Dr. Larry Crabb, *The Silence of Adam*

CONNECTING MEN TO MEN THROUGH CHRIST

A Matter of Choice

"For ye know the grace of our Lord Jesus Christ, that, though he was rich, yet for your sakes he became poor, that ye through his poverty might be rich."
2 Corinthians 8:9

"Let this mind be in you, which was also in Christ Jesus: Who, being in the form of God, thought it not robbery to be equal with God: But made himself of no reputation, and took upon him the form of a servant, and was made in the likeness of men: And being found in fashion as a man, he humbled himself, and became obedient unto death, even the death of the cross."
Philippians 2:5-8

> "THE KIND OF GOD HE IS SHOULD BE THE KIND OF PERSON YOU ARE BECOMING."
> **Dr. Howard Hendricks**

SECTION 10 – INFLUENCE

After approximately three years with Jesus, one important lesson the disciples had learned was the priority He had placed on being a servant. Yet during a private moment with them, shortly before His death, He told them that they had now graduated from just being a servant to a deeper level He called friendship. He would always consider them His most intimate friends—allies on the same side in a cause. Whether we connected in larger groups, smaller groups, or in one-on-one relationships, it would be this same perspective that we would need to rethink and maintain if we were to have any sustaining influence as a men's ministry. Somehow, more of our brothers would have to accept the challenge to be servants as well as mentors, disciplers, and shepherd/leaders. Connecting on these levels, with His word and the Holy Spirit to guide us, it would be great to see God change lives because we were faithful as His friends.

> "Where there is no guidance, a nation falls, but in an abundance of counselors there is safety."
> **Proverbs 11:14 (NRSV)**

CONNECTING MEN TO MEN THROUGH CHRIST

Celebrating a Friendship

"And it came to pass, when he had made an end of speaking unto Saul, that the soul of Jonathan was knit with the soul of David, and Jonathan loved him as his own soul...Then Jonathan and David made a covenant, because he loved him as his own soul. And Jonathan stripped himself of the robe that was upon him, and gave it to David, and his garments, even to his sword, and to his bow, and to his girdle."
1 Samuel 18:1, 3-4

Chemistry

Trust

Commitment

"A true friend is one who hears and understands when you share your deepest feelings...A true friend prods you to personal growth, stretches you to your full potential. And most amazing of all, celebrates your successes as if they were his own."
Richard Exley, *The Making of A Man*

CONNECTING MEN TO MEN THROUGH CHRIST

Philosophy for Changed Lives

"And that from a child thou hast known the holy scriptures, which are able to make thee wise unto salvation through faith which is in Christ Jesus. All scripture is given by inspiration of God, and is profitable for doctrine, for reproof, for correction, for instruction in righteousness: That the man of God may be perfect, thoroughly furnished unto all good works."
2 Timothy 3:15-17

"Likewise, ye younger, submit yourselves unto the elder...."

"But the Helper, the Holy Spirit, whom the Father will send in My name, He will teach you all things, and bring to your remembrance all things that I said to you."
John 14:26 (NKJV)

...Yea, all of you be subject one to another, and be clothed with humility."
1 Peter 5:5a

"You are today what you'll be five years from now, except for the people you meet and the books you read."
Charlie "Tremendous" Jones

CONNECTING MEN TO MEN THROUGH CHRIST

Profile for Shepherd/Leader Mentoring

> Model: Barnabas
>
> Mentor is a wise, experienced friend
>
> Focus: protégé's agenda
>
> Focus: supportive relationship
>
> Focus: whole life counsel
>
> Interchange is based on relationship
>
> Ideally a lifetime commitment
>
> Offers practical life experience
>
> Requires positive personal relationship

From *Mentoring* by Bobb Biehl

CONNECTING MEN TO MEN THROUGH CHRIST

Profile for Shepherd/Leader Discipleship

> Model: Paul and Timothy
>
> Discipler is a teacher/professor
>
> Focus: leader's agenda
>
> Focus: content
>
> Focus: spiritual disciplines
>
> Interchange is based on content
>
> Usually short-term commitment
>
> Offers academic mastery
>
> Requires only respect

From *Mentoring* by Bobb Biehl

CONNECTING MEN TO MEN THROUGH CHRIST

Perception of a Shepherd/Leader

"I am the good shepherd, and know my sheep, and am known of mine. As the Father knoweth me, even so know I the Father: and I lay down my life for the sheep."
John 10:14-15

"Who being the brightness of his glory...

"He who has seen Me has seen the Father."
John 14:9 (NKJV)

and the express image of his person..."
Heb. 1:3

"Be shepherds of God's flock that is under your care, serving as overseers—not because you must, but because you are willing..."
1 Peter 5:2a (NIV)

SECTION 11 – INVOLVEMENT

As I considered the potential of the men within our local church, as well as that of others I might meet along the way from other area churches, I found myself thinking about the limitless possibilities before us if only we would become more intentionally involved as godly men of purpose and influence. I found myself thinking back to our earliest times together as a small group of eight ordinary men, and how even then I could see God was working in each of our hearts. I can vividly recall some of the men literally rising to the edge of their seats as we talked about wanting "something more" from our Christian experience and not being "sure of what that was." Much like Abraham as well as many other Old and New Testament men God called and used to accomplish His purposes, even though we did not know where we were going or how we were going to get there, we were confident in His ability to "get the job done." Again, like many others who had gone before us, we slowly found ourselves wanting to be more involved in "His plans," wanting to make a difference, and wanting to "Rise to God's Call."

> "In the year that King Uzziah died, I saw the Lord sitting on the throne, high and lifted up, and the train of His robe filled the temple...Also I heard the voice of the Lord, saying: 'Whom shall I send, And who will go for Us?' Then I said, 'Here am I! Send me.'"
> **Isaiah 6:1,8 (NKJV)**

CONNECTING MEN TO MEN THROUGH CHRIST

Rising to God's Call

"I beseech you therefore, brethren, by the mercies of God, that ye present your bodies a living sacrifice, holy, acceptable unto God, which is your reasonable service. And be not conformed to this world: but be ye transformed by the renewing of your mind, that ye may prove what is that good, and acceptable, and perfect, will of God."
Romans 12:1-2

Position
Ephesians 2:8-10

Presentation
2 Timothy 2:15

Pursuit
Colossians 3:1, 2

Productivity
2 Peter 1:8

As His Servants and Friends

"Now unto him that is able to keep you from falling, and to present you faultless before the presence of his glory with exceeding joy, to the only wise God our Saviour, be glory and majesty, dominion and power, both now and ever. Amen."
Jude 1:24,25

Connecting Men to Men Through Christ

Pleasing the Father

"But we see Jesus, who was made a little lower than the angels for the suffering of death, crowned with glory and honour; that he by the grace of God should taste death for every man."
Hebrews 2:9

"He is despised and rejected of men; a man of sorrows, and acquainted with grief: and we hid as it were our faces from him; he was despised, and we esteemed him not. Surely he hath borne our griefs, and carried our sorrows: yet we did esteem him stricken, smitten of God, and afflicted. But he was wounded for our transgressions, he was bruised for our iniquities: the chastisement of our peace was upon him; and with his stripes we are healed. All we like sheep have gone astray; we have turned every one to his own way; and the Lord hath laid on him the iniquity of us all...Yet it pleased the LORD to bruise him; he hath put him to grief..."
Isaiah 53:3-6,10

"For it became him, for whom are all things, and by whom are all things, in bringing many sons unto glory, to make the captain of their salvation perfect through sufferings. For both he that sanctifieth and they who are sanctified are all of one: for which cause he is not ashamed to call them brethren, Saying, I will declare thy name unto my brethren, in the midst of the church will I sing praise unto thee."
Hebrews 2:10-12

Hallelujah! What a Savior!

CONNECTING MEN TO MEN THROUGH CHRIST

A Defining Moment

"But Peter, standing up with the eleven, lifted up his voice, and said unto them, Ye men of Judaea, and all ye that dwell at Jerusalem, be this known unto you, and hearken to my words."
Acts 2:14

"Men of Israel, hear these words: Jesus of Nazareth, a Man attested by God to you by miracles, wonders, and signs which God did through Him in your midst, as you yourselves also know Him, being delivered by the determined purpose and foreknowledge of God, you have taken by lawless hands, have crucified, and put to death; whom God raised up, having loosed the pains of death, because it was not possible that He should be held by it... Therefore let all the house of Israel know assuredly that God has made this Jesus, whom you crucified, both Lord and Christ."... Then Peter said to them, "Repent, and let every one of you be baptized in the name of Jesus Christ for the remission of sins; and you shall receive the gift of the Holy Spirit."...Then those who gladly received his word were baptized; and that day about three thousand souls were added to them."
Acts 2:22-24, 36, 38, 41 (NKJV)

"If any man speak, let him speak as the oracles of God; if any man minister, let him do it as of the ability which God giveth: that God in all things may be glorified through Jesus Christ, to whom be praise and dominion for ever and ever. Amen."
1 Peter 4:11

CONNECTING MEN TO MEN THROUGH CHRIST

A Divine Appointment

"And I thank Christ Jesus our Lord, who hath enabled me, for that he counted me faithful, putting me into the ministry; Who was before a blasphemer, and a persecutor, and injurious: but I obtained mercy, because I did it ignorantly in unbelief."
1Timothy 1:12-13

The Audience

"And I said, Who art thou, Lord? And he said, I am Jesus whom thou persecutest. But rise, and stand upon thy feet: for I have appeared unto thee for this purpose, to make thee a minister and a witness both of these things which thou hast seen, and of those things in the which I will appear unto thee."
Acts 26:15-16

The Adventure

"Delivering thee from the people, and from the Gentiles, unto whom now I send thee, To open their eyes, and to turn them from darkness to light, and from the power of Satan unto God, that they may receive forgiveness of sins, and inheritance among them which are sanctified by faith that is in me."
Acts 26:17-18

CONNECTING MEN TO MEN THROUGH CHRIST

A Divine Appointment
(Continued)

The Arena

"For we preach not ourselves, but Christ Jesus the Lord; and ourselves your servants for Jesus' sake. For God, who commanded the light to shine out of darkness, hath shined in our hearts, to give the light of the knowledge of the glory of God in the face of Jesus Christ."
2 Corinthians 4:5-6

> "What I really lack is to be clear in my mind what I am to do, not what I am to know…the thing is to understand myself, to see what God really wishes me to do…to find the idea for which I can live and die."
>
> **Soren Kierkegaard**

CONNECTING MEN TO MEN THROUGH CHRIST

Contemplating the Call

"Wherefore also we pray always for you, that our God would count you worthy of this calling, and fulfil all the good pleasure of his goodness, and the work of faith with power: That the name of our Lord Jesus Christ may be glorified in you, and ye in him, according to the grace of our God and the Lord Jesus Christ."
2 Thessalonians 1:11-12

Chasing the Wind

"And whatsoever mine eyes desired I kept not from them, I withheld not my heart from any joy; for my heart rejoiced in all my labour: and this was my portion of all my labour. Then I looked on all the works that my hands had wrought, and on the labour that I had laboured to do: and, behold, all was vanity and vexation of spirit, and there was no profit under the sun."
Ecclesiastes 2:10-11

Field of Dreams

"Jesus saith unto them, My meat is to do the will of him that sent me, and to finish his work…Lift up your eyes, and look on the fields; for they are white already to harvest."
John 4:34, 35b

Faith and Service

"And Jesus answered them, saying, The hour is come, that the Son of man should be glorified. Verily, verily, I say unto you, Except a corn of wheat fall into the ground and die, it abideth alone: but if it die, it bringeth forth much fruit. He that loveth his life shall lose it; and he that hateth his life in this world shall keep it unto life eternal. If any man serve me, let him follow me; and where I am, there shall also my servant be: if any man serve me, him will my Father honor."
John 12:23-26

CONNECTING MEN TO MEN THROUGH CHRIST

A Matter of Perspective

"But we have this treasure in earthen vessels, that the excellency of the power may be of God, and not of us. We are troubled on every side, yet not distressed; we are perplexed, but not in despair; persecuted, but not forsaken; cast down, but not destroyed; always bearing about in the body the dying of the Lord Jesus, that the life also of Jesus might be made manifest in our body."
2 Corinthians 4:7-10

"...I have set before thee an open door, and no man can shut it..."
Rev. 3:8a

"For God's gifts and the calling of God are irrevocable"
Romans 11:29
(NKJV)

"Him that overcometh will I make a pillar in the temple of God..."
Rev. 3:12

"For which cause we faint not; but though our outward man perish, yet the inward man is renewed day by day. For our light affliction, which is but for a moment, worketh for us a far more exceeding and eternal weight of glory; while we look not at the things which are seen, but at the things which are not seen: for the things which are seen are temporal; but the things which are not seen are eternal."
2 Corinthians 4:16-18

SECTION 12 – INSTRUMENTS

As God was moving us along, we could see that there was good steady progress and growth taking place on an individual level and the team level, as well as within the overall ministry. The ministry was attracting both younger and older men, but in particular was generating a strong interest among those men with young families. This was an encouraging sign, as the daily struggles for the men in this age group are so intense, and their need to be connected to other committed Christian brothers is so urgent. As we were maturing, we were becoming more and more aware of just how essential it was that we would train ourselves to be godly instruments in His hand, and once prepared for service, be willing to enter the fight for the hearts of those men within our "sphere of influence." Standing together for Jesus Christ, as a group of committed men, was and would continue to be an obligation, a privilege, and an honor.

> "…he will be an instrument for noble purposes, made holy, useful to the Master and prepared to do any good work."
> **2 Timothy 2:21b (NIV)**

CONNECTING MEN TO MEN THROUGH CHRIST

Visions and Dreams

"And it shall come to pass in the last days, saith God, I will pour out of my Spirit upon all flesh: and your sons and your daughters shall prophesy, and your young men shall see visions, and your old men shall dream dreams... And it shall come to pass, that whosoever shall call on the name of the Lord shall be saved."
Acts 2:17, 21

The Cause

The Camaraderie

The Convictions

"Lay not up for yourselves treasures upon earth, where moth and rust doth corrupt, and where thieves break through and steal: but lay up for yourselves treasures in heaven, where neither moth nor rust doth corrupt, and where thieves do not break through nor steal: for where your treasure is, there will your heart be also."
Matthew 6:19-21

CONNECTING MEN TO MEN THROUGH CHRIST

Standing Together

"So we make it our goal to please him..."
2 Corinthians 5:9 (NIV)

As Fathers

As Husbands

As Sons

As Brothers

As Soldiers

"...stand firm in all the will of God, mature and fully assured."
Colossians 4:12b (NIV)

"On reviewing the facts of my life, I discovered a marvelous truth: I have never done anything important outside the context of a team."
Bob Buford, *Halftime*

CONNECTING MEN TO MEN THROUGH CHRIST

Preparing for Battle

"And every man that striveth for the mastery is temperate in all things. Now they do it to obtain a corruptible crown; but we an incorruptible."
1 Corinthians 9:25

Authentic

Leaders

Equipped

Reliable

Trained

"Discipline yourselves, keep ALERT. Like a roaring lion your adversary the devil prowls around, looking for someone to devour. Resist him, steadfast in your faith, for you know that your brothers and sisters in all the world are undergoing the same kind of suffering."
1 Peter 5:8-9 (NRSV)

"Therefore prepare your minds for action; discipline yourselves; set all your hope on the grace that Jesus Christ will bring you when he is revealed."
1 Peter 1:13

"The more effective the leadership, the greater the price that must be paid."
Chuck Swindoll

CONNECTING MEN TO MEN THROUGH CHRIST

Fulfilling His Purpose

"To the intent that now unto the principalities and powers in heavenly places might be known by the church the manifold wisdom of God, According to the eternal purpose which he purposed in Christ Jesus our Lord."
Ephesians 3:10-11

You are the
Salt
of the Earth
Matthew 5:13

You are the
Light
of the World
Matthew 5:14

THEREFORE

> "Don't waste your life. You only get one crack at it."
> **John Piper**

"Give therefore thy servant an understanding heart to judge thy people, that I may discern between good and bad: for who is able to judge this thy so great a people? And the speech pleased the Lord, that Solomon had asked this thing."
1 Kings 3:9-10

SECTION 13 – INFILTRATION

By this time, countless hours had been spent together planning and praying, friendships had deepened, numerous books had been read, and a great amount of training had already taken place. I sensed that God's vision, to this point, had been communicated clearly, carefully, and in a timely manner. A solid foundation for an effective ministry to men was in place from which we could all build and benefit. More opportunities were now available for us to reach out to men with the gospel message of Jesus Christ so that men could get saved and equipped to serve Him. As we would "enter the arena" onto " the playing field" in new ways, so to speak, we understood it would require greater faith, obedience, and sacrifice from each one of us. Anticipating that the road ahead would, at times, be more difficult and the battle more intense than ever before, it would force us to advance on our knees, in God's power, as a team united and focused on His glory at all times.

> "And see, now I go bound in the spirit to Jerusalem, not knowing the things that will happen to me there, except that the Holy Spirit testifies in every city, saying that chains and tribulations await me."
> **Acts 20:22-23 (NKJV)**

CONNECTING MEN TO MEN THROUGH CHRIST

Entering the Arena

"For it seems to me that God has put us apostles on display at the end of the procession, like men condemned to die in the arena."
1 Corinthians 4:9a (NIV)

"And I, brethren, when I came to you, did not come with excellence of speech or of wisdom declaring to you the testimony of God. For I determined not to know anything among you except Jesus Christ and Him crucified. I was with you in weakness, in fear, and in much trembling. And my speech and my preaching were not with persuasive words of human wisdom, but in demonstration of the Spirit and of power, that your faith should not be in the wisdom of men but in the power of God."
1 Corinthians 2:1-5

"'Ah, Lord God! Behold, You have made the heavens and the earth by Your great power and outstretched arm. There is nothing too hard for You."
Jeremiah 32:17 (NKJV)

"The size of your God determines the size of your faith."
Donald Grey Barnhouse

Connecting Men to Men Through Christ

Engaging the Opposition

"Finally, my brethren, be strong in the Lord, and in the power of his might. Put on the whole armor of God, that ye may be able to stand against the wiles of the devil. For we wrestle not against flesh and blood, but against principalities, against powers, against the rulers of the darkness of this world, against spiritual wickedness in high places."
Ephesians 6:10-12

"Now thanks be unto God, which always causeth us to triumph in Christ, and maketh manifest the savor of his knowledge by us in every place. For we are unto God a sweet savor of Christ, in them that are saved, and in them that perish: to the one we are the savor of death unto death; and to the other the savor of life unto life. And who is sufficient for these things?"
2 Corinthians 2:14-16

"And such trust have we through Christ to God-ward: not that we are sufficient of ourselves to think any thing as of ourselves; but our sufficiency is of God; who also hath made us able ministers of the new testament; not of the letter, but of the spirit: for the letter killeth, but the spirit giveth life."
2 Corinthians 3:4-6

If we distrust our cause, or our leader, or our armor, we give the devil an advantage.
Matthew Henry

Encountering the Opposition

"And David said to Saul, Let no man's heart fail because of him; thy servant will go and fight with this Philistine. And Saul said to David, Thou art not able to go against this Philistine to fight with him: for thou art but a youth, and he a man of war from his youth."
1 Samuel 17:32-33

> "O Lord, I bless thee that the issue of the battle between thyself and Satan has never been uncertain, and will end in victory. Give me such fellowship with thee that I may defy Satan, then shall my hand never weaken, my feet never stumble, my sword never rest, my shield never rust, my helmet never shatter, my breastplate never fall, as my strength rests in the power of thy might."
> **Arthur Bennett, *The Valley of Vision***

"Then said David to the Philistine, Thou comest to me with a sword, and with a spear, and with a shield: but I come to thee in the name of the Lord of hosts, the God of the armies of Israel, whom thou hast defied...And all this assembly shall know that the Lord saveth not with sword and spear: for the battle is the Lord's, and he will give you into our hands."
1 Samuel 17:45, 47

CONNECTING MEN TO MEN THROUGH CHRIST

Enduring the Opposition

"Thou therefore endure hardness, as a good soldier of Jesus Christ. No man that warreth entangleth himself with the affairs of this life; that he may please him who hath chosen him to be a soldier."
2 Timothy 2:3-4

"But recall those earlier days when, after you had been enlightened, you endured a hard struggle with sufferings, sometimes being publicly exposed to abuse and persecution, and sometimes being partners with those so treated...Do not, therefore, abandon that confidence of yours; it brings a great reward. For you need endurance, so that when you have done the will of God, you may receive what was promised."
Hebrews 10:32-33, 35-36 (NRSV)

"But without faith it is impossible to please him: for he that cometh to God must believe that he is, and that he is a rewarder of them that diligently seek him."
Hebrews 11:6

Oh for a faith that will not shrink!

CONNECTING MEN TO MEN THROUGH CHRIST

Faith...Obedience...Sacrifice

"For I am persuaded, that neither death, nor life, nor angels, nor principalities, nor powers, nor things present, nor things to come, Nor height, nor depth, nor any other creature, shall be able to separate us from the love of God, which is in Christ Jesus our Lord."
Romans 8:38-39

"Wherefore seeing we also are compassed about with so great a cloud of witnesses...who through faith subdued kingdoms, wrought righteousness, obtained promises, stopped the mouths of lions, quenched the violence of fire, escaped the edge of the sword, out of weakness were made strong, waxed valiant in fight, turned to flight the armies of the aliens. Women received their dead raised to life again: and others were tortured, not accepting deliverance; that they might obtain a better resurrection: and others had trial of cruel mockings and scourgings, yea, moreover of bonds and imprisonment: they were stoned, they were sawn asunder, were tempted, were slain with the sword: they wandered about in sheepskins and goatskins; being destitute, afflicted, tormented; of whom the world was not worthy: they wandered in deserts, and in mountains, and in dens and caves of the earth. And these all, having obtained a good report through faith, received not the promise: God having provided some better thing for us, that they without us should not be made perfect."
Hebrews 12:1a, 11:33-40

"All men die...Few men ever really live."
John Eldredge, *Wild at Heart*

CONNECTING MEN TO MEN THROUGH CHRIST

Exiting the Arena

"Go to now, ye that say, To day or to morrow we will go into such a city, and continue there a year, and buy and sell, and get gain: Whereas ye know not what shall be on the morrow. For what is your life? It is even a vapour, that appeareth for a little time, and then vanisheth away."
James 4:13-14

"For this we say unto you by the word of the Lord, that we which are alive and remain unto the coming of the Lord shall not prevent them which are asleep. For the Lord himself shall descend from heaven with a shout, with the voice of the archangel, and with the trump of God: and the dead in Christ shall rise first: then we which are alive and remain shall be caught up together with them in the clouds, to meet the Lord in the air: and so shall we ever be with the Lord. Wherefore comfort one another with these words."
1 Thessalonians 4:15-18

"See then that ye walk circumspectly, not as fools, but as wise, redeeming the time, because the days are evil. Wherefore be ye not unwise, but understanding what the will of the Lord is."
Ephesians 5:15-17

SECTION 14 – INTROSPECTION

Someone once said "the longer the battle, the more intense the struggle," and, together as a team, that has been our experience. In particular, as the primary ministry coordinator, I have had and continue to have my share of Satan's attacks. Let me remind us all that, in view of the vast potential within us as Christian men, Satan will do whatever he can to try to keep us "on the sidelines," uninvolved as godly role models/leaders among those we love and are able to influence most. Even though we might be united in heart as Christian brothers, he would have us divided in our efforts, fighting our battles alone, and in our own strength. Furthermore, if he can convince us that simply "showing up" and being "nice guys" is enough, we will never experience the joy that can be ours if we would assume our God-given responsibilities. As we are Christ's ambassadors, "voices in the wilderness," we are always guaranteed His presence. And as we labor together as "men in the arena," let us never forget that we were bought with the price of the precious blood of Jesus Christ. In the busyness of life may we remind ourselves daily regarding "who we are" and "whose we are," that we would finish our individual races well.

> "Now then, we are ambassadors for Christ, as though God were pleading through us: we implore you on Christ's behalf, be reconciled to God. For He made Him who knew no sin to be sin for us, that we might become the righteousness of God in Him."
> **2 Corinthians 5:20-21 (NKJV)**

CONNECTING MEN TO MEN THROUGH CHRIST

Finishing the Race

"I have fought a good fight, I have finished my course, I have kept the faith."
2 Timothy 4:7

> "All God's giants have been weak men, who did great things for God because they reckoned on His power and presence to be with them."
> **Hudson Taylor**

> "My greatest fear is being successful at things that don't matter."
> **Author Unknown**

"Therefore, my beloved brethren, be ye stedfast, unmoveable, always abounding in the work of the Lord, forasmuch as ye know that your labour is not in vain in the Lord."
1 Corinthians 15:58

> "God's work done in God's way will never lack God's supply."
> **Hudson Taylor**

CONNECTING MEN TO MEN THROUGH CHRIST

Reflecting on the Mission

"Our work is not to save souls, but to disciple them. Salvation and sanctification are the work of God's sovereign grace, and our work as His disciples is to disciple others' lives until they are totally yielded to God. One life totally devoted to God is of more value to Him than one hundred which have simply been awakened by His Spirit."
Oswald Chambers

"It is not the critic who counts, not the man who points out how the strong man stumbles, or where the doer of deeds could have done them better. The credit belongs to the man in the arena, whose face is marred by dust and sweat and blood, who strives valiantly...who knows the great enthusiasms, the great devotions, who spends himself in a worthy cause, who at best knows in the end the triumph of high achievement, and who at the worst, if he fails, at least fails while daring greatly, so that his place shall never be with those cold and timid souls who have never known neither victory or defeat."
Teddy Roosevelt

CONNECTING MEN TO MEN THROUGH CHRIST

Delivering the Message

"There was a man sent from God, whose name was John. The same came for a witness, to bear witness of the Light, that all men through him might believe. He was not that Light, but was sent to bear witness of that Light."
John 1:6-8

"He must increase...

"He said, I am the voice of one crying in the wilderness, Make straight the way of the Lord, as said the prophet, Isaiah."
John 1:23

...but I must decrease."
John 3:30

"Or do you not know that your body is the temple of the Holy Spirit who is in you, whom you have from God, and you are not your own? For you were bought at a price; therefore glorify God in your body and in your spirit, which are God's."
1 Corinthians 6:19-20 (NKJV)

"Remember who you are and whose you are...God has a very special plan for your life."
Ron Hostetler, *There is No Joy in Gruntsville*

CONNECTING MEN TO MEN THROUGH CHRIST

A Personal Decision

"...choose you this day whom you will serve...but as for me and my house, we will serve the Lord."
Joshua 24:15

"For God so loved the world, that he gave his only begotten Son... that whosoever believeth in him should not perish, but have everlasting life."
John 3:16

"I am the way, the truth, and the life: no man cometh unto the Father, but by me."
John 14:6

"I am the resurrection, and the life: he that believeth in me, though he were dead, yet shall he live."
John 11:25

"Therefore if any man be in Christ, he is a new creature: old things are passed away; behold, all things are become new."
2 Corinthians 5:17

CONNECTING MEN TO MEN THROUGH CHRIST

A Difference Maker

The Voice of a Team

"Neither pray I for these alone, but for them also which shall believe on me through their word; That they all may be one; as thou, Father, art in me, and I in thee, that they also may be one in us: that the world may believe that thou hast sent me."
John 17:20-21

"Although the force of one person fully committed to God is tremendous, it pales in comparison to the force of God's people moving together. While never violating our uniqueness, we move together, united in heart and soul. Our greatness is unleashed in the context of community. When we move together, God is most perfectly revealed in us."
Erwin Raphael McManus, *The Barbarian Way*

"I am the Vine, you are the branches."
John 15:5a

"So teach us to number our days, that we may apply our hearts unto wisdom...And let the beauty of the LORD our God be upon us: and establish thou the work of our hands upon us; yea, the work of our hands establish thou it."
Psalm 90:12,17

SECTION 15 – ILLUMINATION

As I share my concluding thoughts with you, at the time of this printing some of us are now several months into our fourth year together. Once again, I've just finished my time of annual reflection upon the present state of the ministry in terms of what God has accomplished thus far, where we are currently, and what is next according to His timetable. As He grows His ministry, new opportunities will become available for personal growth and ministry as God raises up additional men who are willing to be equipped to serve Him as "a man in the arena." For each of us, the challenge continues that we would be men who make God's plans our prayer and priority, who work hard, stay focused in our hearts, invest in the eternal, and finish our journey well. With the possibility of someday soon either standing or kneeling around the throne "Before an Audience of One," may it be our heart's desire to hear the voice of our Lord and Savior Jesus Christ reply…"Well done my good and faithful servant." What would be a better time than now to make your faith decision to "Rise to God's Call" as part of a team?

> "When I was a child, I spake as a child, I understood as a child, I thought as a child: but when I became a man, I put away childish things. For now we see through a glass, darkly, but then face to face…we shall be like him; for we shall see him as he is."
> **1 Corinthians 13:11-12a, 1 John 3:2b**

CONNECTING MEN TO MEN THROUGH CHRIST

Beginning the Connection

"And Jesus, walking by the sea of Galilee, saw two brethren, Simon called Peter, and Andrew his brother, casting a net into the sea: for they were fishers. And he saith unto them, Follow me, and I will make you fishers of men. And they straightway left their nets, and followed him."
Matthew 4:18-20

"...and saw two ships standing by the lake: but the fishermen were gone out of them, and were washing their nets. And he entered into one of the ships, which was Simon's, and prayed him that he would thrust out a little from the land. And he sat down, and taught the people out of the ship. Now when he had left speaking, he said unto Simon, Launch out into the deep, and let down your nets for a draught. And Simon answering said unto him, Master, we have toiled all the night, and have taken nothing: nevertheless at thy word I will let down the net. And when they had this done, they inclosed a great multitude of fishes: and their net brake. And they beckoned unto their partners, which were in the other ship, that they should come and help them. And they came, and filled both the ships, so that they began to sink."
Luke 5:2-7

"Be still, and know that I am God."
Psalm 46:10

"And Jesus said unto Simon, Fear not; from henceforth thou shalt catch men. And when they had brought their ships to land, they forsook all, and followed him."
Luke 5:10b-11

CONNECTING MEN TO MEN THROUGH CHRIST

Completing the Connection

"To whom also he shewed himself alive after his passion by many infallible proofs, being seen of them forty days, and speaking of the things pertaining to the kingdom of God...but wait for the promise of the Father, which, saith he, ye have heard of me."
Acts 1:3, 4b

"Now upon the first day of the week, very early in the morning, they came unto the sepulchre, bringing the spices which they had prepared, and certain others with them. And they found the stone rolled away from the sepulchre. And they entered in, and found not the body of the Lord Jesus. And it came to pass, as they were much perplexed thereabout, behold, two men stood by them in shining garments: and as they were afraid, and bowed down their faces to the earth, they said unto them, Why seek ye the living among the dead? He is not here, but is risen: remember how he spake unto you when he was yet in Galilee, saying, The Son of man must be delivered into the hands of sinful men, and be crucified, and the third day rise again. And they remembered his words..."
Luke 24:1-8

"So then the Lord Jesus, after he had spoken to them, was taken up into heaven and sat down at the right hand of God. And they went out and proclaimed the good news everywhere, while the Lord worked with them and confirmed the message by the signs that accompanied it."
Mark 16:19-20 (NRSV)

CONNECTING MEN TO MEN THROUGH CHRIST

Leaving a Legacy

"Greater love hath no man than this, that a man lay down his life for his friends."
John 15:13

What was it about Jesus Christ that captured the hearts of his disciples, uniting them as a team in an unwavering commitment to Him, though their loyalty would eventually cost them their lives? Was it how he was thought of while he was alive or was it how he was remembered after he died? Of course, for them as it should be for us, it would be both. Despite any opposition that awaited them, they could say with deep affection and confidence that Jesus was their Master, they were His friends, and at the beginning and end of each day, that is all that mattered.

> "A man is no fool who gives what he cannot keep to gain what he cannot lose."
> **Jim Elliot**

CONNECTING MEN TO MEN THROUGH CHRIST

Rejoicing in Hope

"Blessed be the God and Father of our Lord Jesus Christ, which according to his abundant mercy hath begotten us again unto a lively hope by the resurrection of Jesus Christ from the dead, to an inheritance incorruptible, and undefiled, and that fadeth not away, reserved in heaven for you, who are kept by the power of God through faith unto salvation ready to be revealed in the last time. Wherein ye greatly rejoice, though now for a season, if need be, ye are in heaviness through manifold temptations: that the trial of your faith, being much more precious than of gold that perisheth, though it be tried with fire, might be found unto praise and honor and glory at the appearing of Jesus Christ: whom having not seen, ye love; in whom, though now ye see him not, yet believing, ye rejoice with joy unspeakable and full of glory: receiving the end of your faith, even the salvation of your souls."
1 Peter 1:3-9

CONNECTING MEN TO MEN THROUGH CHRIST

Before the Throne

"...they cast their crowns before the throne..."
Revelation 4:10b (NRSV)

" And I beheld, and I heard the voice of many angels round about the throne, and the beasts, and the elders: and the number of them was ten thousand times ten thousand, and thousands of thousands; saying with a loud voice, Worthy is the Lamb that was slain to receive power, and riches, and wisdom, and strength, and honor, and glory, and blessing. And every creature which is in heaven, and on the earth, and under the earth, and such as are in the sea, and all that are in them, heard I saying, Blessing, and honor, and glory, and power, be unto him that sitteth upon the throne, and unto the Lamb for ever and ever. And the four beasts said, Amen. And the four and twenty elders fell down and worshipped him that liveth for ever and ever."
Revelation 5:11-14

"And, behold, I come quickly; and my reward is with me, to give every man according as his work shall be. I am Alpha and Omega, the beginning and the end, the first and the last."
Revelation 22:12-13

CONNECTING MEN TO MEN THROUGH CHRIST

INTERVENTION
Rise Up, O Men of God!

1. Rise up, O men of God!
   Have done with lesser things.
   Give heart and mind and soul and strength
   to serve the King of kings.

2. Rise up, O men of God!
   The kingdom tarries long.
   Bring in the day of brotherhood
   and end the night of wrong.

3. Rise up, O men of God!
   The church for you doth wait,
   her strength unequal to her task;
   rise up, and make her great!

4. Lift high the cross of Christ!
   Tread where his feet have trod.
   As brothers of the Son of Man,
   rise up, O men of God!

William P. Merrill, 1911

"Who will rise up for me against the evildoers? or who will stand up for me against the workers of iniquity?"
Psalm 94:16

Recommended Reading

Wild at Heart; Waking the Dead, by John Eldredge
No Man Left Behind, by Patrick Morley, David Delk, and Brett Clemmer
Man in the Mirror; The Seven Season's of a Man's Life, by Patrick Morley
Tender Warrior; Four Pillars of a Man's Heart; Locking Arms, by Stu Weber
Halftime, by Bob Buford
Called to be God's Leader, by Henry and Richard Blackaby
Anointed to be God's Servants, by Henry and Richard Blackaby
The Warrior's Heart, by Harry R. Jackson
There Is No Joy In Gruntsville, by Ron and Jeff Hostetler
Why Men Hate Going To Church, by David Murrow
Ablaze for God, by Wesley L. Duewel
Lead Like Jesus, by Ken Blanchard and Phil Hodges
Twelve Ordinary Men, by John MacArthur
The Barbarian Way; Chasing Daylight, by Erwin Raphael McManus
The Fisherman, by Larry Huntsperger
The Master Plan of Evangelism, by Robert E. Coleman
Rising to the Call, by Os Guinness
Living Water, by Brother Yun
Search and Rescue, by Neil Cole
If You Want to Walk on Water You've Got to Get Out of the Boat, by John Ortberg
The Silence of Adam, by Dr. Larry Crabb
Standing Together, by Howard Hendricks
God's Ground Force, by Barbara Sullivan

About the Author

Larry Garland currently coordinates "Connecting Men to Men," a growing Christian men's ministry at his local church. Seven years ago, God began developing his heart to shepherd men at the local church level, and this book is a product of his experience and his desire to inspire other men to godly lifestyles that honor Jesus Christ.

Larry was born and raised in York, Pennsylvania, and continues to reside there with his wife of thirty-four years, Bonnie. They attend the Church of the Open Door along with their son, David; his wife, Angela; and grandson, Jonah. They also have a daughter, Lindsay, who works and resides in the Washington DC area.

Additional Information

By now you probably realize that this is not a typical book that should be read in a typical way, but it is a book that could be reflected upon from time to time. Properly used, it could serve as a great source of encouragement to "raise the bar" in your personal walk with Jesus Christ and inspire other Christian men to do the same.

For more information about the "Connecting Men to Men" ministry, or for more information about how to obtain additional copies of this book, you can email Larry Garland at:

cmm2005@comcast.net